CREATIVE
STENCILING
&
DECORATIVE TECHNIQUES

CREATIVE
STENCILING
& DECORATIVE TECHNIQUES

CLB

First published in Great Britain in 1999 by
Michael O'Mara Books Limited
9 Lion Yard
Tremadoc Road
London SW4 7NQ

5154 Creative Stenciling
Copyright © L'Aventurine, Paris, 1998
Copyright © Michael O'Mara Books Limited, 1999
for the English-Language Edition

This edition published in 1999 by CLB
A division of Quadrillion Publishing Ltd,
Godalming Business Centre, Woolsack Way,
Godalming, Surrey, GU7 1XW, UK

Distributed in the United States by Quadrillion Publishing, Inc.
230 Fifth Avenue, New York, NY 10001

ISBN 1-84100-163-5

1 3 5 7 9 10 8 6 4 2

Typeset by K DESIGN, Winscombe, Somerset

Printed in Singapore by Tien Wah Press PTE Ltd

CONTENTS

INTRODUCTION

If you enjoy expressing your creative talents with imagination and flair, then the art of stenciling is perfect for you. This fast, effective, easy-to-learn technique produces the most dramatic and stylish effects, with the minimum of effort. You don't need to be an accomplished artist either – stenciling allows you to reproduce the same motif over and over again with complete accuracy. Stenciled motifs are wonderfully effective whether they are used in simple or complex designs, and the variety of ways in which they can be used is endless.

Stenciling is surprisingly flexible too. You'll quickly discover how to apply motifs, friezes, patterns and scenes onto a wide range of surfaces, including wood, fabric, paper, cardboard, metal, terracotta and china. Just look around your home – there is infinite scope for using this exciting, versatile skill. Whether you want to freshen up your lampshades and drapes, or create smart, stylish stationery personalized just for you, you'll discover a treasure trove of ideas for using stencils creatively and enjoyably. Stenciling is a direct, simple way of giving your home and possessions a brand new look – so don't throw things out, stencil them instead! You can also make clever, original gifts for friends and family, each stamped with your personal touch!

In *Creative Stenciling*, you will find everything you need to learn this fun, creative technique. Step-by-step instructions, advice on equipment and invaluable handy tips are detailed throughout, helping you to achieve trouble-free success. After experimenting with a selection of mixed media projects, you can then progress to more specialized projects, using a dazzling array of inspirational, inventive and colorful stencil designs for boxes, paper and fabric. The generous selection of illustrations in the Motif section of the book is so irresistible you'll want to begin at once! So start stenciling now – all the scope you need to create truly delightful designs is provided here.

MIXED MEDIA PROJECTS

EQUIPMENT

Here is a list of the equipment you'll need for the basic projects on pages 14–28. Many of these will come in useful for the other projects in this book. Check the list of equipment for each project for more specific ingredients.

For drawing and cutting out

- An HB pencil

- A white eraser

- A ruler, preferably metal, to use as a cutting guide

- A T-square

- A roll of masking tape

- A utility knife

- A pair of scissors

- An artist's craft knife with spare blades

- A cutting mat, a wooden board, or a sheet of glass (for a cutting surface)

- Tracing paper

- Smooth, heavy-weight watercolor paper

- Smooth, lightweight watercolor paper

- Acetate sheets or plastic stencil film for photocopying

For painting

- Use stenciling brushes: the flat, straight end of the brush makes it easy to cover surfaces evenly.

- Flat, square-ended graining brushes in several widths

- A small sponge paint roller, with spare rolls

- A kitchen sponge

- A small bottle of linseed oil that has been simmered in a double boiler for 8 minutes from when the water boils. You can use this oil to waterproof stencils made from watercolor paper by applying a coat on just one side of a lightweight stencil paper or on both sides of a thicker paper. (Or, pre-oiled stencil board.)

- A spray-can of repositional remount adhesive

- A wire brush

- Fine-grade sandpaper

- Reusable sticky notes

Paints

Different kinds of paint are suitable for different kinds of surface.

1 Artists' oil paints can be diluted with turpentine. However, they are seldom used for stenciling because they take so long to dry. It is possible to reduce the drying time by diluting the paint with matte varnish or acrylic varnish.

2 Artists' acrylics are water-soluble and dry quickly to form an indelible plastic film. This enables you to apply several coats in quick succession. Brushes must be washed as soon as you have finished using them. They can also be soaked in water. If you allow them to dry, it becomes impossible to get the paint off them.

3 Fabric paints are usually sold in bottles or jars and can be used like watercolor paints. You must take care not to get too much fabric paint on the brush because it can be very runny and flow under the stencil. Once the paint is dry, you can fix the design onto the fabric by ironing over it, protecting the motif with a thin cloth. Once the paint is fixed, the fabric can be washed at a maximum of 140°F, but this can be risky. Always read through the manufacturer's instructions carefully before using any fabric paint.

4 Ceramic paints are difficult to use, not because they are tricky to handle, but because they often have to be fired at very high temperatures that cannot be reached using an ordinary domestic oven.

5 To protect your stencils more effectively, you can apply a layer of 'one-coat' latex paint to it with a brush.

Patinas and varnish

- Gilder's bole. This brick-colored fine clay pigment is the traditional base coat used for gilding on wood or pottery. You apply it with a cloth, your finger, or a small brush.

- Antique restorers' gilding cream comes in a jar. You can rub it on with a cloth.

- Black patina is used by antique restorers and comes in the same form as the gilding cream. It can be applied using a cloth, your finger, or a fine brush.

- Crackle medium

- Antiquing varnish

- Gloss varnish

- Matte varnish for oils

- Spray varnish

MAKING STENCILS

There are two steps to making stencils. The first consists of preparing and cutting out the motifs you have selected. The second involves applying the paint to the object of your choice.

A few techniques for making your stencils

Cutting out stencils

1 Trace your chosen motif onto smooth lightweight watercolor paper that you have already waterproofed with linseed oil (see page 10). This weight of paper is suitable for small and intricate motifs. For larger simple motifs you can use heavy-weight paper.

2 You can also use photocopying acetate for your stencil. This special plastic film comes in sheets and is available from large art or craft supply stores. Try and get the thickest quality available. You can photocopy your motif directly onto the plastic and then cut it out.

3 Alternatively, you can photocopy your motif onto a sheet of paper, stick the photocopy to smooth watercolor paper, and cut out the two sheets together, to obtain your stencil.

When cutting out stencils, use a cutting mat to protect your surface. This 're-heals' itself once cut and lasts a long time. It is also durable and retains a clean, smooth surface. Otherwise use a wooden board or a sheet of glass.

Artists' craft knives: these are available from supply stores and are essential for cutting out intricate stencils. Use them with care, however, and store them safely!

DON'T FORGET!

Cutting out a simple motif from your chosen material to make a stencil is easy and straight-forward. However, cutting out a complex motif can be more complicated and you may need to create 'bridges' to join the various parts of the stencil design together (see the illustration opposite). Allow a sufficient number of regularly-spaced bridges depending on the design. Protect your stencil, if it is made out of watercolor paper, with a coat of latex paint. Once your stencil is dry and hardened by the paint, it is ready for use.

A few useful tips

- Your chosen stencil paint shouldn't be too runny or too dry.

- Practice stenciling on some scrap paper before you embark on the real thing.

- It's more practical to pour some paint onto a plate, saucer, or palette, rather than to dip your brush directly into the paint container. This helps you to prepare the right amount of paint for the tool you are using and the effect you wish to achieve. It also allows you to work with a wide palette of colors, mixing them as required.

- Never overload your brush painting tool, and dab the paint thinly over the stencil so that it does not run underneath.

- To prevent the stencil from slipping, it should be fixed in place with some masking tape. If the stencil is made of a thin, flexible material like plastic film you can spray it underneath with some repositional remount.

- Choose the appropriate tool for the type of stencil you are using:
  - A small graining brush for small, intricate motifs
  - Brushes or paint pads for larger designs
  - Rollers or sponges for creating different patinas.*

* This is used for an aging technique to give a surface a gray-green appearance.

bridge

Lampshades come into their own in the evening, casting a warm, friendly glow. As you can see in the picture, plain shades can be stenciled to achieve very different styles.

1 Trace a few simple motifs from the Motif section that will be easy to cut out. Then transfer them onto paper or photocopy them onto an acetate sheet. Cut the stencils out with a craft knife. Decide how you want to arrange the motifs around the lampshade. Measure the distance between each one so that you can space them evenly. Once you have decided where they will go, mark the motif positions on the lampshade with reusable sticky notes.

2 Position the stencils on the shade and secure them in place with masking tape. Pour some fabric paint into dishes that will enable you to scrape your brush and control the amount of paint you are applying to the fabric. Apply the paint thinly using a flat-ended round stencil brush with very short, fine bristles. Allow plenty of time for the paint to dry thoroughly.

3 Remove the stencil and make sure it's completely dry before repositioning it for the next motif. If desired, to help your stencil stick to the fabric of the lampshade, spray the back of it with some repositionable remount adhesive. To give the design an 'aged' effect, you can apply the paint very lightly or unevenly. You can also produce a fainter, more delicate motif by using a brush that is almost dry.

HANDY TIPS!

The conical shape of a lampshade is not very convenient for applying large stencils, so keep them small.

Painting stencils on a lampshade is tricky because fabric paint can be runny and therefore more likely than other paint to stain surfaces. Work on a well-protected surface.

Do not heat the lampshade to fix the paint.

STATIONERY

Decorative stationery, whether it is subtle and discreet or flamboyant and daring, reflects the personality of its creator. Use stencil effects to personalize your letters, decorate your notebooks and brighten your life!

1 Once you have decided what you are going to decorate, you can create a design using either a single large stencil to fill the area, or several smaller stencils that you can arrange however you like to make a pattern. Simple themes like animals, flowers, or leaves can be used to produce very attractive compositions, whether they are arranged geometrically or at random.

2 Cut out the stencil designs you have chosen from oiled stencil board, waxed stencil paper, waterproofed watercolor paper, or plastic stencil film. Then assemble the stationery items you want to personalize: writing paper and envelopes, diaries, notebooks, notepads, etc. You can even create your own albums and book covers. To do this, you need some heavy-weight rag paper or watercolor paper.

3 Paint your stencil motifs using acrylic paint, which is simple to use, and can be easily mixed into the desired colors. Stick to simple color-schemes. When you are painting a porous material like rag or watercolor paper, you don't need a varnish glaze. However, on a notebook cover, for example, you may want to give a shiny finish for design purposes; this can be done by applying a gloss varnish with a brush. Give the varnish plenty of time to dry, then apply a second coat to even out the paint layers.

HANDY TIPS!

It's great fun to make your own notebooks. You can simply hole-punch sheets of paper and bind them together with ribbon.

Or, you could sew the pages together using a big darning needle and some thick thread or kitchen string.

Use rough or dainty stitching depending on the artistic effect you want to achieve.

Frames look wonderful decorated with stencils. Scatter them all around your home and use them to experiment with different design effects – it's a great way of trying out your latest creative ideas. They make perfect gifts for all your friends too!

1 There are several ways of making decorative frames. If you want a varnished frame, you need to prepare the painting surface to make it non-porous, so that the varnish adheres better. Sand the wood, apply an undercoat of primer, sand again, then apply your chosen shade of varnish. You can also leave the frame as it is and instead decorate a *passe-partout* mat (available from art supply stores) with your stencil design.

2 Cut out a few small paper or plastic stencils and attach them to the frame with masking tape. Use acrylic paints and experiment with different effects; you can fill in your motifs with an artist's brush using different colors (see, for example, the frame decorated with animals), or dab on different patterns and colors with a stencil brush (the frame decorated with flower sprigs gives you an illustration). You can also use one or more type of brush and a range of different colors.

3 When your stencils are completely dry, use a small roller to apply a coat of either matte or gloss varnish. Make sure the varnish is evenly distributed and there are no air bubbles. Alternatively, apply the varnish gently with a hog-hair brush, always smoothing it in the same direction.

HANDY TIPS!

Preferably, you should choose simple, flat frames. If there is a slant, the stencil is more difficult to position and blobs of paint are likely to form underneath it.

To give your frame an 'aged' look, scrape the stenciled designs gently with a wire brush or some fine-grade sandpaper to lift off a bit of the paint in a few areas of each motif. Then varnish.

Trays are perfect for serving drinks, or for carrying objects from room to room. Give your trays a touch of unique style with stenciled motifs.

1 Measure the inside base of your tray and cut out a piece of thin, firm pressed-paper board of the same size. The board should be of a fairly heavy weight so that it doesn't curl up once painted.

Trace a very simple background pattern (a line of parallel stripes for example) onto the board with a ruler and pencil. Next, mix some acrylic paint on a plate or saucer and fill in your pattern with a fine brush. Allow to dry thoroughly.

2 Choose motifs from the Motif section and make your stencils. Mark the positions of your stencils with some reusable sticky notes. If you have several stencils or if you want to reproduce the same stencil several times, the stickers will help you place them accurately and won't leave any marks when they are removed.

If you are creating a large motif, paint your first color from right to left, using a small paint pad. To create a graduated effect, dip your pad or brush into the color once only and allow the paint to run out as you reach the edge of the stencil. Let dry a second time.

You can then add some luster by applying a second color on top of the first, shading off in the opposite direction with a fine brush.

3 To give an antique appearance to your tray, use a crackle medium. Once your motif is completely dry, apply two or three coats of matte varnish in order to smooth out any areas of thick paint. Ensure that the varnish is evenly distributed over the whole surface of the motif. Allow to dry thoroughly between each coat.

Apply a first coat of crackle medium, distributing it well in all directions using a hog-hair brush. Smooth it out, using the right amount of pressure. Leave to harden until the surface seems dry when you brush your finger over it. Apply a second coat. Don't forget that the longer you allow the first coat of varnish to dry, the more successful the crackled effect will be. Allow ten days for the varnish to dry completely.

In order to emphasize the cracks, squeeze some oil paint out of the tube (a sepia color or a gray for example) directly onto a clean rag. Apply the paint using a circular motion, so that it gets into all the cracks. Wipe off the surplus very gently with a soft, dry rag. Finally, stick your stenciled design to the tray.

HANDY TIPS!

You could stick wallpaper to the tray as a base, choosing a stripe or a plain or an imitation wood grain in the color of your choice.

Buy one or two tubes of artists' oil paint for a crackling effect. The colors are fabulous.

You can age your tray in the same way as your design, which will make the whole thing look a treat!

Fresh, country-style china looks so bright and welcoming in the home. You can experiment with lots of different stencil styles and bring your plain white dishes to life!

1 As you need special equipment for firing ceramic paint, you could try using food coloring. This is less durable, of course, but it will enable you to recreate the design shown here quite easily. Two motifs, a duck and a hen, are used to create matching variations on a single theme. This technique of arranging two small motifs in a variety of ways can be used for all kinds of projects on all kinds of objects. The choice of motif and style is limitless!

2 Cut your stencils from a sheet of plastic stencil film – this is essential because the shape of china makes rigid stencils difficult to use. Decide on the positioning of your stencils and stick them to the china with masking tape or spray the stencils with repositional remount adhesive. Use a combination of different motifs or repeat the same one several times, using your own imagination. Paint your motif with ceramic paint or food coloring. Then paint an identical band on the whole set, using a roller.

HANDY TIPS!

To try your hand at painting china, you could buy a set of inexpensive white pottery to practice the basic techniques.

If you use ceramic paint, it should be fired in workshops equipped with kilns – ask in your art supply store for help with locating one.

If you choose food coloring, protect it with a coat of varnish that is not water-soluble.

Do not eat off china decorated in this way; use it for decorative purposes only.

TEA TOWELS

Fabric is an ideal surface for decorating with stencils. Why not start with some simple tea towels? The examples shown here illustrate how you can use decorative friezes and panels to create colorful and dramatic effects with fabric paints.

1 You can create lovely designs with stenciled patterns on fabrics. Here are a few examples of how you can personalize your tea towels. Look in the Motif section – you need to choose a motif that you can repeat several times, linking each one to the last to form a frieze. Transfer the chosen design onto waxed stencil paper or photocopy it onto thick plastic film. Cut out the stencil. It's a good idea to make some spares because you will be using lots of repeats in this project.

2 Gently spray a little repositional remount adhesive onto the back of your stencil and stick it to the fabric (remount adhesive doesn't stain). Dip a round stencil brush lightly into the fabric paint and dab it over the motif, taking care to completely fill the shape (each type of fabric will require a different amount of paint).

3 To emphasize your motif, you can create several friezes or perhaps add some colored stripes, using one or several colors for your design. You can also create a graduated effect by starting with a light shade and gradually adding some darker color as you work toward the center. Then continue to dab on the dark color, gradually eliminating the lighter color until you obtain the dark color on its own. Either work from light to dark or from dark to light. Make sure you rinse your brush regularly so that the color changes rapidly. Leave the fabric to dry and then pass an iron over it to fix the color, while protecting the motif with a cloth.

HANDY TIPS!

Use special fabric paints. They are fairly runny and can be a bit tricky to handle. When you are applying them, put just a small amount on the brush and make sure that the stencil is stuck down firmly to the fabric.

Allow the paint to dry well before retouching or applying another color.

Once you have finished you need to iron the cloth, to help the paint to penetrate into the textile fibers. (Be sure to read the manufacturer's instructions for the fabric paints before beginning the stenciling).

PAILS & WATERING CANS

Here's your chance to brighten up your metal pails and watering cans and make gardening an even greater pleasure. Stenciled motifs on metal surfaces look really stylish, and they are not difficult to apply.

1 To help the paint adhere to the metal surface, lightly sand it down with some fine-grade sandpaper and apply a matte varnish. Then mix your choice of acrylic colors on a plate. Three or four shades will be enough. Use a different brush for each of the colors to keep them clean. Cut your stencil from thick plastic stencil film, and spray the back of the stencil with some repositional remount adhesive (this will help the stencil to stick well for several paint applications). Once the varnish is dry, you are ready to apply your stencil.

2 For extra grip, you can also use some masking tape to secure your stencil. Give free rein to your imagination as you arrange your colors and blend the layers one after another without following any particular plan. The only precaution you must take is to allow the paint to dry thoroughly between coats. You can start by applying the main color with a paint pad. Then as you gradually get down to the fine detail, you will need increasingly finer brushes.

3 Repeat exactly the same process several times, repositioning the stencil each time. Take care not to stick a stencil onto a painted area, even if the paint is dry. For parts that are difficult to get at or when the main stencil cannot be used due to the curved surface, prepare some separate, smaller stencils that will adhere more easily. Using smaller motifs also makes it easier to control paint application on deeper curves.

HANDY TIPS!

When using acrylic from a tube don't over-dilute it with water. Try to maintain a thick or medium consistency, especially if your cutouts are very intricate.

POTS & FLOWERPOT-HOLDERS

Terra-cotta flowerpots have never looked so stylish! Just look at the stunning effects that we've created with these pretty stenciled designs.

1 Cut some stencils from thick plastic stencil film: choose arabesques, leaves, stripes, spots, etc. Keep the stencils small as pots are usually conical in shape which makes it difficult to stick on the stencils. Spray the back of the stencils with repositional remount adhesive or use masking tape.

Try several effects – a gold patina, for example, applied in two stages. Once you have fixed your stencil in place, first apply some gilder's bole (see page 11) with your finger or a small brush. Once it's dry, apply a gilding cream on top with your finger and allow to dry. If you like, polish it to a shine using a rag or soft brush.

2 You can also try a black patina which is applied in exactly the same way as the brick-colored gilder's bole (see page 11). Or, for more varied effects, combine the three substances, using one, two, or three at a time. Always allow time for the terra-cotta to absorb the layers thoroughly. Stripes can be marked with masking tape.

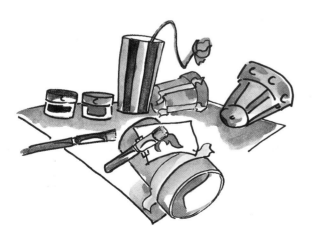

3 Gilder's bole and gold and black patina are all very easy to use. However, remember not to apply them too thickly. Apart from that any color combination goes: tone on tone, terra-cotta and brick, terra-cotta with brick and gold on top, terra-cotta with black, or even black or brick over gold. You will discover all kinds of possibilities as you go along, using this special technique which allows you lots of scope.

HANDY TIPS!

If the pots are to be used as flowerpots, it's best to use slightly diluted acrylic paint. But they can also be turned into very decorative flowerpot-holders, utensil-holders, or storage jars.

To place a single flower in a pot, stick it into a piece of florists' foam.

BEAUTIFUL BOXES

Boxes are so useful – in fact they are essential if you don't have much storage space in your home. They enable you to hide away all the irritating clutter that accumulates in your life. In this chapter, you will discover that boxes can be beautiful, as well as practical! These inspired projects show you a host of ways to personalize boxes in styles that are fresh, original, and charming. Just look at all the different boxes that you have around the house – shoe boxes, file boxes, stationery boxes, small boxes containing Christmas or business cards – you'll be amazed how quickly and easily, and with how little effort, they can be transformed into pretty, decorative objects.

If you don't have many boxes, start hoarding right now – and make sure you collect a variety of shapes, sizes, and materials. Alternatively, you could buy some from stationery stores or large stores specializing in home furnishing and decorating.

There are all kinds of boxes to decorate in the following projects, including brilliantly colorful toy boxes, charming keepsake boxes, and stylish file boxes. Also, you'll be using varying techniques to create a satisfying range of artistic effects. Simply follow the instructions and tips that accompany each project, and choose your favorite motifs from the Motif section – soon you'll be creating your very own designs!

BEAUTIFUL BOXES PROJECTS

EQUIPMENT

The tools and materials below will be invaluable in helping you achieve complete success in making the individual projects shown on the following pages.

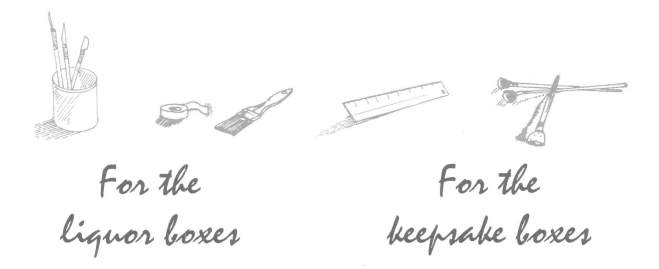

For the liquor boxes

- Plain, unvarnished thin pine boxes

- A medium-size flat brush

- Artists' acrylics

- Acetate for photocopying or plastic stencil film

- A craft knife with spare blades

- A cutting mat

- A spray can of repositional remount adhesive

- An engraving tool for scoring lines

- A pair of scissors

- Very fine-grade sandpaper

- Matte varnish

For the keepsake boxes

- A set of different-sized plain cardboard boxes

- A pair of scissors

- A spray can of repositional remount adhesive or low-tack masking tape

- An HB pencil

- A can of lighter fluid

- A small wooden spatula or spoon

- Cotton balls

For the mini storage drawers

- A small plain, unvarnished thin pine box with drawers
- A medium-size flat brush
- Artists' acrylics
- Matte varnish
- Masking tape
- Ready-to-use crack filler
- A small plastic spatula
- A fine brush

For the carnival toy boxes

- Cardboard boxes
- An HB pencil
- Low-tack masking tape
- Artists' acrylics
- A medium-size flat brush
- Tracing paper
- A can of lighter fluid
- Cotton balls
- A wooden spatula or spoon
- A fine brush
- Matte or gloss varnish

For the big toy boxes

- Wooden boxes (empty wine crates, for example)
- A drill and wood bits
- Medium-grade sand paper
- Artists' acrylics
- A 2-inch-wide sponge paint roller
- A metallic silver felt-tip marker
- Thin pressed-paper board
- A spray-can of repositional remount adhesive or low-tack masking tape
- A can of lighter fluid
- Cotton balls
- A wooden spatula or spoon
- A sheet of thin metal
- A craft knife with spare blades
- Adhesive
- Upholstery or shoe tacks

For the file boxes

- File boxes in thin plain, unvarnished pine, or thick, firm cardboard
- A kitchen sponge
- Acetate or plastic stencil film for photocopying

- A craft knife with spare blades

- A cutting mat

- Artists' acrylics

- A round flat-ended stenciling brush

- Satin varnish

- A spray-can of repositional remount adhesive

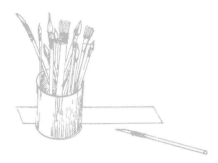

For the garden boxes

- Cardboard boxes

- Self-adhesive paper

- An HB pencil

- Masking tape

- A can of lighter fluid

- Cotton balls

- A wooden spatula or spoon

- Water-based paint (gouache or water-colors)

- Artists' acrylics

- A can of artists' fixative spray (the type used for fixing charcoal pencils)

For the heirloom boxes

- Wooden box with a lid

- A kitchen sponge

- Various grades of sandpaper – medium, fine, very fine

- Satin and matte varnishes

- Coloring pigments

- A fine brush

- A medium-size soft brush

- A pair of nail scissors or an artist's craft knife with spare blades

- Polyvinyl acetate glue

- Oil-based varnish

THE TECHNIQUES NEEDED

Liquor boxes: stenciling, etched lines
Keepsake boxes: transfers
Mini storage drawers: patterns etched into a filler base
Carnival toy boxes: painted transfers
Big toy boxes: transfers
File boxes: stenciling
Garden boxes: transfers and watercolor
Heirloom boxes: varnished collage

A few useful tips

- You don't have to buy everything brand new, you can salvage boxes that you can decorate and personalize later.

- Buy the art materials in small quantities because the craft projects included are all relatively small.

- An artist's craft knife is the best choice for accurate cutting. It is impossible to get the same result with scissors!

- When applying transfers with lighter fluid, you should do a test first because certain materials don't lend themselves very well to this technique. Try out the technique on a few surfaces before beginning your project.

- Never completely soak the photocopied motifs in lighter fluid – simply moisten them lightly on the back.

- Avoid applying transfers to glossy or (film-covered) surfaces because the transferred motifs will not adhere to them.

- Avoid preparing a large amount of acrylic paint because once it dries it is unusable.

 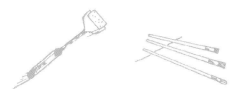

LIQUOR BOXES

These impressive liquor boxes have a quiet touch of class – and make great storage boxes for your glasses and decanters. With their distinctive striped surfaces and classic motifs, they provide a stylish welcome for your friends.

1 Choose plain, unvarnished pine boxes and dust them off with a dry brush. Then wipe them with a damp sponge to remove any remaining dirt.

Mix some acrylic paint in a small bowl to create the color you want to use. Use a thick consistency, only slightly diluted with water, and mix enough for a single coat.

Trace or photocopy your motifs onto a sheet of acetate or plastic stencil film, then carefully cut them out with a craft knife.

Prepare one motif for each side of the box, and one for the lid, preferably from the same theme. Alternatively, use the same motif throughout. Lightly spray some repositional remount adhesive onto the back of the motifs and stick them onto the box. Position one motif in the center of each side and one on the center of the lid.

2 Using a medium-size brush, quickly apply a thick coat of paint to one side of your box, covering the whole surface, including the motif. Then, before the paint dries completely, take a sharp pointed tool (such as an engraving tool, awl, the tip of a nail file, or the tip of a pair of nail scissors) and scrape away the paint in horizontal lines, uncovering the wood underneath.

Carefully peel off the stencil, using a needle or the tip of your craft knife.

Let the paint dry, then repeat the process on the remaining sides.

3 Once the box is completely painted and dry, accentuate the stripes by scoring them a second time, using an engraving tool or any implement with a fine, sharp point (see above). Using a piece of fine-grade sandpaper, sand the corners of the box and lid, rubbing them very gently to define the edges.

As a finishing touch, varnish each box and lid with matte varnish. Leave the box to dry completely (a day or two) before using.

HANDY TIPS!

To obtain a neat, smooth painted surface, it's a good idea to sand down any rough areas on the box before decorating it.

Cut out the acetate motifs on a cutting mat or a wooden board.

To score straight, even stripes, use a metal ruler as a guide for your engraving tool.

We all have letters and little notes that we like to read again and again – they evoke so many memories! Whether you have a collection of old love letters, notebooks, travel journals, or souvenir albums, these keepsake boxes will keep all your treasures safe.

1 Cardboard boxes are available in all shapes and sizes and a variety of colors. For this project, try to find boxes made from cardboard that has a fairly rough, porous, and natural rather than glossy surface. Look for a few boxes in different sizes that you can use to create a matching set.

Choose a style of decoration that contrasts well with the cardboard – an architectural theme for example.

Make a few black and white photocopies of the motifs, enlarging them as necessary, depending on the size you want to transfer onto the box.

In this example, we have centered the motif on the lid.

2 Cut out the photocopied motifs, taking care to leave a wide margin around the edge of the motif design.

Find the middle of the lid of your box and center the motif, face down. Secure the motif by attaching it at the corners with low-tack masking tape. Alternatively, spray repositional remount adhesive onto the corners in the margin around the motif and press the corners down lightly. Take care to avoid getting any adhesive on the photocopied image.

3 Moisten a cotton ball with lighter fluid and gently wipe it over the back of the motif. Make sure you cover the entire image. Then quickly press down the photocopy, applying equal pressure all over. When the paper is almost dry, rub it up and down with a wooden spatula, pressing firmly to transfer the motif. Carefully lift up one corner to check if the transfer has been successful. If it isn't perfect, repeat the process a second time. Be careful not to move the photocopy! If you prefer, you can leave the motif only partially transferred for an antique effect.

Lift off the photocopy, and leave the transfer to dry.

HANDY TIPS!

If you use masking tape, make sure it is low-tack masking tape so that it doesn't tear the surface of the box when you remove it.

Before applying the transfer to your box, test a spare motif on a cardboard scrap to make sure the image is perfectly clear once transferred.

MINI STORAGE DRAWERS

A miniature dresser is perfect for storing your pencils, crayons, artists' brushes, erasers, and other odds and ends. With a touch of creativity, it can be transformed from a plain box into something warm, personal, and stylish.

1 For this project, you need a small dresser in plain, unvarnished pine. Wipe the dresser inside and out with a slightly damp sponge to remove any dust.

Mix some acrylic paint in a small bowl to create the color you want to use. Alternatively, you can use a diluted fabric dye if you want to let the grain of the wood show through. Take a medium-size flat brush and apply one coat of color all over the dresser, including the drawers. Clean the brush. When the acrylic paint is dry, use the brush to coat the box with a matte varnish. Leave to dry thoroughly.

2 To create the pattern on the drawers, begin by masking the border area around the front of the drawers. This will ensure neat, straight edges.

Next, put some fine crack filler in a small saucer. Apply the filler smoothly with a small plastic spatula, completely covering the area inside the masking.

3 Draw your motif by etching the design freehand with the handle of a paint brush, a match, or any item with a sharp point, depending on how thick you want your lines to be. Do this as soon as you have applied the filler; you must not allow it to dry out. As you work, remove the filler that builds up on the end of the tool. Lastly, remove the masking tape and leave to dry completely.

HANDY TIPS!

If you want to show the wood grain, you can use a diluted fabric dye, but read the manufacturer's instructions carefully.

For a tinted filler, mix in some gouache diluted with water.

To vary the texture of the filler, you can mix in other substances such as sand, salt, fine sawdust, etc. Always spread the filler with a flexible spatula.

CARNIVAL TOY BOXES

These decorated boxes have a happy carnival atmosphere and are just perfect for storing away all those tiny, precious toys. Paint bold, bright stripes in contrasting colors and add some amusing stenciled alphabet letters – the effect is delightful!

1 With your pencil, draw bands approximately 1 inch wide and 2 inches apart around the sides of each round box and across the lid. Mask some of the bands with low-tack masking tape. Mix some brightly colored acrylic paint, diluting it in a small dish. Using a flat medium-size brush, paint the box and leave to dry; then remove the tape. Choose the motifs you want to use and photocopy them, enlarging if necessary to the size you want. If the motif is a letter or number, photocopy it onto tracing paper, then reverse the image by placing the tracing paper on the photocopier with the motif right side up, in order to obtain a negative photocopy. When you transfer the reversed number or letter onto the box it will be the right way round.

2 Cut out the photocopied motifs leaving a 1 inch margin around each one and place them face down on the unpainted areas of the box. Secure them lightly with low-tack masking tape. Moisten a cotton ball with lighter fluid and gently wipe it over the back of the motif, covering the entire image. Quickly press down the photocopy, applying equal pressure allover. When the paper is almost dry, rub a spatula up and down over the back of it, pressing firmly to transfer the motif. Lift up one corner slightly to check if the transfer has been successful. If it isn't perfect, repeat the process a second time. Be careful not to move the photocopy! Lastly, remove the masking tape, lift off the photocopy, and leave to dry.

3 Using a fine brush, and bright shades of acrylic paint, color the motifs. Leave until completely dry. Then apply several coats of matte or gloss varnish. Let the varnish dry for one hour between coats.

HANDY TIPS!

If your box is porous enough and the stripes made with diluted acrylics, the transfer will adhere over the paint. Test on a scrap before beginning your project. You can decorate any shape of box with this technique.

If you come across any wooden boxes or crates, add them to your empty-box collection. They make good, sturdy storage chests for children's toys, and they look exceptionally bright and cheerful when decorated with imagination and a touch of humor.

1 To prepare your box, pull out any protruding nails with pliers. Sand down any splintered or rough areas on the wood. Decide whether you want to make handles. If you want to be able to carry the box, drill two holes in the center of two opposite sides for rope handles (see Handy Tips). If you want to pull the box out like a drawer, drill holes in one side only. Use a piece of sandpaper to smooth any wood splinters.

Next, mix some acrylic paint on a plate. The paint should be very slightly diluted. Using 2-inch-wide sponge paint roller, paint some stripes onto the outside of the box. Leave to dry.

Using a metallic silver felt-tip marker, draw one or several thin stripes down the edges and the middle of your broad painted stripes. Set the box aside to dry.

2 Next, make the label. To do this, first photocopy some silhouette motifs to transfer onto a rectangle of thin pressed-paper board approximately 4 inches by 7 inches, depending on the size of the box. Spray a touch of repositional remount adhesive onto the margin of the photocopy in the corners and place the photocopy face down on the board. Press the corners down lightly. Lightly moisten a cotton ball with lighter fluid and wipe it over the back of the images. Then rub the back of the photocopy with a wooden spatula and remove it. Leave to dry.

3 Take a sheet of thin metal and cut out a rectangle approximately 1 inch larger overall than the card label. Make a rectangular window in the metal sheet by cutting out the middle section with a craft knife. Dab a line of adhesive along the edges on the back of the metal frame. Stick the frame onto the printed label, making sure the label is positioned at the center. Bend the surplus metal to the back of the label. Finally, fix it to your box with upholstery or shoe tacks, and attach the handles (see Handy Tips).

HANDY TIPS!

If you can't get a sheet of thin metal from your craft supply store, use heavy-duty aluminum foil instead, but careful it doesn't get crumpled.

You can fit all sorts of handles to the box: door handles, cupboard handles, and drawer handles. Or, you can drill holes and attach knotted ropes or ribbons.

GASTON BERNHEIM DE V...

PETITES HIS...

GRANDS

Jazz up your shelves with these prettily decorated file boxes. They are perfect for hiding away anything from magazines to music scores.

1 You can use thin plain unvarnished pine file boxes, or thick, firm cardboard file boxes available from stationery stores.

Clean the surfaces and remove any dust with a dry brush or a damp sponge.

Choose a motif that you can reproduce again and again, such as leaves or geometric shapes. Photocopy or trace your motif onto a sheet of acetate or plastic stencil film. Then carefully cut out the motif on a cutting mat, using a craft knife.

2 Mix your chosen acrylic colors in some small glass bowls or saucers, graduating the shades by adding extra white acrylic to produce five different shades. If you are using acrylic from a tube, dilute it only very slightly – it is best to work with thick paint when you are dabbing it onto a stencil.

Spray a touch of repositional remount adhesive onto the back of the stencil and stick it onto the wood. Start with the lightest shade. Using a stenciling brush and very little paint, gradually fill in the stencil. Remove the stencil and leave the paint to dry. Continue with the same color until the box is partially covered.

Apply the other shades in turn, using a darker shade each time, so that your stencils overlap the motifs that are already dry. Gradually fill in the decoration as the color gets darker. When you have finished, you will have a beautifully graduated effect with the same motif partially or completely covering the wood.

3 Once the motifs are completely dry, apply a first coat of satin varnish. Leave this to dry until the surface is no longer tacky, then apply a second coat. Leave to dry for at least 24 hours. Repeat the process applying successive coats of the satin varnish until you no longer feel any surface texture because of the thickness of the paint.

HANDY TIPS!

The simpler your motif, the easier it will be to scatter it all over the surface in a variety of shades.

When applying the paint, it's best to begin with the lightest shade and end with the darkest, so the motifs painted on earlier don't show through.

GARDEN BOXES

Perfect for the garden storeroom, these pretty boxes look as fresh as spring. They are also wonderfully useful for keeping your tools and accessories safe. At last there's somewhere to put all those packets of seeds, twine, tiny pots, and other small gardening odds and ends.

1 For this project, you could use a matching set of colored boxes to achieve a coordinated effect. Otherwise use old shoe boxes, or similar containers.

First if you are using recycled boxes, cover them with plain or patterned self-adhesive paper (a small check pattern is pretty, or try plain brown parcel paper). When they are covered, draw a rectangle in the center of the lid. This will help you decide on the size of the motif and the margins around it.

2 Choose some sketches of flowers or plants from the old botanical illustrations in the Motif section. Photocopy them, enlarging them or reducing them, depending on how big a space you have marked out on the boxes.

Once all your motifs have been selected and photocopied in the correct size, cut them out leaving a wide margin around the edge of each motif. Next, place the motifs face down on the lids and secure them with masking tape at each corner.

Moisten a cotton ball with lighter fluid and wipe it over the back of the image. Make sure you cover the entire motif. Gently rub the back of the photocopy with a wooden spatula.

3 Detach the photocopies, then color in the motifs with a wash using a palette of water-based paints. Let the paint dry. Lastly, finish off the fine details in acrylic paint.

Spray the completed design with aerosol fixative (the kind used for charcoal pencils) and leave to dry.

HANDY TIPS!

You can cover the boxes with paper that isn't self-adhesive. Just spray the back of the paper with repositional remount adhesive first. Don't choose glossy paper because the surface won't absorb the ink when you apply your transfer – instead, as you smooth down the transfer, the ink diluted with the lighter fluid will form blotches.

HEIRLOOM BOXES

If you are lucky enough to have an old cigar box, here is your chance to restore it. Decorated cigar boxes lend an elegant air to the home. They are wonderfully nostalgic and the perfume from their wood delights everyone who opens them.

1 Salvage an old cigar box, or any other good quality wooden box with a lid. If necessary, wipe the box inside and out with a damp sponge to remove any loose dust.

Sand it gently with successive sheets of medium, fine, and very fine sandpaper, to obtain a beautifully smooth, even surface.

Remove the dust from sanding with a dry brush and then a damp sponge.

Once the surfaces are clean and the wood taken back to its natural state, you can prepare your varnish.

2 To tint the wood, use a clear satin varnish with some pigment mixed into it. In this example we have used burnt umber.

Pour the varnish into a small container. Take up a small amount of pigment on a thin brush, sprinkle it onto the varnish and then stir until it is completely blended. The more pigment you add, the darker the color will be.

Apply a coat of your tinted varnish to the box with a medium-size soft brush. Leave to dry for two hours and repeat the process until you have a thick, smooth, dry coat in the desired color.

3 Once you have chosen a theme and motifs, cut the motifs out with a craft knife or pair of nail scissors, carefully preserving every fine detail. Before you apply the motifs, use your cutouts to experiment with different layouts.

Each motif must be stuck down perfectly to prevent any air bubbles from forming. Using a thin brush, spread some adhesive on the back of each motif, covering the entire piece of paper. Position the motif right side up on the box and press down firmly. Leave to dry.

Next, varnish the box with a matte varnish, completely covering the motifs. Apply ten coats with 30 minutes drying-time between each one. Make sure you wait long enough for the varnish to dry, before you add the next coat. Finally apply several coats of oil-based varnish (wait 24 hours between each coat). Leave to dry for an entire week.

HANDY TIPS!

To create layers of varnish that are smooth and even, always use a very flexible brush, and brush on the varnish firmly so it makes a good, smooth surface. Remove any surface bubbles as you work. Leave each coat to dry completely before adding another so that the surface doesn't warp or crack.

PRECIOUS PAPERS

Paper is used for a host of applications, from letters and invitations to wrapping presents and even decorating walls. In this chapter, you can learn how to decorate paper quickly and easily using a variety of different artistic effects and for a range of purposes. You can personalize your gift wrapping, create your own invitations, line the shelves of your closets or dresser drawers with paper covered in original motifs, and even produce your own wallpaper!

This chapter contains some really inspirational ideas on decorating all kinds of paper. These range from regular brown parcel paper and watercolor paper to specialist Japanese papers, decorated with such techniques as embossing, painting, transferring designs, and engraving. All you need to do is follow the instructions and tips that accompany each project and choose your favorite motifs from the Motif section – soon you will be creating your very own designs!

PRECIOUS PAPERS PROJECTS

EQUIPMENT

Here is a list of the essential tools and materials that you will need to decorate your paper as shown on the following pages.

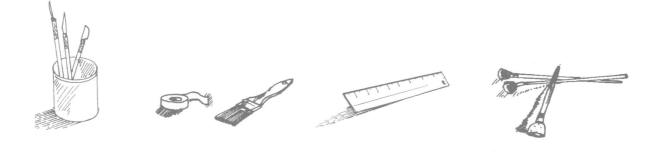

For the embossed writing paper

- An HB pencil

- Thick pressed-paper board or firm cardboard

- A craft knife with spare blades

- Thick, absorbent writing paper and envelopes

- An embossing tool or wooden spoon

For the Japanese writing paper

- Writing paper and envelopes made from onionskin, flower-petal paper, or other Japanese paper

- A pair of scissors

- Low-tack masking tape

- Cotton balls

- A can of lighter fluid

- A wooden spoon or spatula

- A very fine brush

- India ink: black, midnight blue, or violet

- Matte varnish

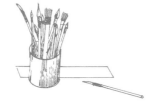

For the marbled gift-wrapping paper

- Large sheets of marbled paper

- A pair of scissors

- An HB pencil

- Low-tack masking tape

- Cotton balls

- A can of lighter fluid

- A wooden spoon or spatula

- White watercolor paint

- A fine brush

- A can of artists' fixative spray (the type used for fixing charcoal pencils)

For the craft wrapping paper

- Craft paper in different colors

- A pair of scissors

- Low-tack masking tape

- Cotton balls

- A can of lighter fluid

- A wooden spatula

- Watercolor paint

- A fine watercolor brush

- A can of artists' fixative spray (the type used for fixing charcoal pencils) or matte water-based varnish

For the gift bags

- Some paper bags (plain or brown)

- A pair of scissors

- Low-tack masking tape

- Cotton balls

- A can of lighter fluid

- A embossing tool or wooden spatula or spoon

- Artists' acrylics

- A fine brush

- Felt-tip markers

- A can of artists' fixative spray (the type used for fixing charcoal pencils)

For the engraved gift tags

- Sheets of glazed paper or thin pressed-paper board

- Artists' acrylics

- A medium-size brush

- Glass paints

- A small sponge

- A calligraphy pen

- A rag

For the paper ribbons

- Large sheets of recycled paper

- A pair of scissors

- Some thumbtacks or push pins

- A wooden board

- Gouache paint – wine-colored, beige, mid-brown, and sepia

- Gold acrylic paint

- A soft brush

- A rag

- Tracing paper

- A thick, soft pencil

- A fine brush

- Fine-grade sandpaper

- A can of artists' fixative spray (the type used for fixing charcoal pencils)

A few useful tips

- Salvage all kinds of paper bags, such as brown paper bags, bags with handles, and little paper packets. You can recycle them all by decorating them and putting them to a new use.

- When it comes to buying paper, buy some basic kinds to begin with, such as big sheets of brown paper and plain paper.

- Use the weight and texture of the paper to obtain different effects.

- Once you have familiarized yourself with the techniques described, you can then go on to decorate some more sophisticated papers, such as striped, marbled, or printed papers.

- If you want to transfer motifs onto your paper, do a test on a sample first to check how well it absorbs the ink. If the paper is quite porous (for example, construction paper) it will quickly soak up the ink diluted with the lighter fuel. If your paper is smooth, and therefore less porous (for example, brown paper), allow the lighter fluid to evaporate before pressing down your photocopy, so that the ink does not smudge.

- When you are applying transfers using tracing paper or lighter fluid, secure your paper to a wooden board or piece of cardboard with some masking tape to keep it stretched out flat.

- Always let your work dry thoroughly between each stage.

THE TECHNIQUES NEEDED

Embossed writing paper: embossing
Japanese writing paper: inked transfers
Marbled gift-wrapping paper: painted transfers
Craft wrapping paper: painted transfers
Gift bags: transfers
Engraved gift tags: pen engraving
Paper ribbons: painted motifs

EMBOSSED WRITING PAPER

You will be proud to put pen to paper once you have created some stylish stationery using this simple technique.

1 Choose a motif composed of shapes that are simple and easy to cut out. Copy it onto thick pressed-paper board or cardboard. Then cut out the motif using a craft knife.

Choose the writing paper and envelopes that you want to emboss. Watercolor paper with a rough texture is often the easiest to work with, and it absorbs moisture quite well which is important for the embossing to work.

2 Boil a pan of water to produce clouds of steam, then soften the sheet of watercolor paper you want to emboss by holding it over the pan.

Place the paper over your cardboard template and rub your finger gently over this area to mark the position of the embossing.

Using an embossing tool or the rounded end of an artist's brush, pencil, or wooden spoon, slowly press the paper into the mold.

3 You may need to steam the paper again to re-soften it, so that you can continue embossing. Use a pencil to make a positioning mark if you are going to move the motif several times. Make sure that the paper is correctly positioned over the mold each time to obtain a really clear impression.

HANDY TIPS!

Try this technique on some envelopes, greetings cards or thick paper tags to create either a single impression or a border.

You can complete the embossing in several stages as long as the paper is kept damp.

The best kind of paper to use is thick watercolor paper.

JAPANESE WRITING PAPER

Create some luxurious and distinctive personalized stationery using Japanese paper and a selection of oriental-style designs.

1 Choose some writing paper and envelopes that are made from Japanese paper, such as onionskin or flower-petal paper. Then select a few oriental motifs, such as the ones featured here.

Photocopy the motifs, enlarging them as necessary to the size you want to use to personalize your stationery. Be careful not to use motifs that are too small and intricate because when you come to paint them with ink, they would not be easy to fill in accurately.

2 Carefully cut out the photocopied motifs, leaving a margin around the edges. Then secure each motif to your writing paper, right side down, with some low-tack masking tape.

Moisten a cotton ball with a little lighter fluid and wipe it over the photocopy. Rub over the back of the motif immediately with a wooden spatula, pressing down hard on the photocopy. Repeat the process, if necessary, to get a really clear transfer, ensuring that you don't move the photocopy as you are doing this.

Then lift up the photocopy and check that the motif has transferred to the paper and that it is dry.

3 Using a very fine brush and some India ink, either black, midnight blue, or violet, carefully paint over the transferred motifs to darken them. Take your time with this delicate work – you have to be accurate so that the motif stands out clearly on the paper.

Let the ink dry completely, then cover the motif with several coats of matte varnish, letting each coat dry for half an hour before applying the next. Leave to dry.

HANDY TIPS!

If you choose delicate paper like onionskin or tissue, secure your sheet to a piece of firm cardboard with some low-tack masking tape before transferring the motifs. This will prevent it from creasing or tearing.

MARBLED GIFT-WRAPPING PAPER

Create a little nostalgia by transferring some charming traditional motifs onto marbled paper. You can then use this to wrap gifts or to cover notebooks and boxes.

1 Choose large sheets of marbled paper and select some old Victorian-style motifs. Decide what size you want the motifs to be and photocopy some of them, enlarging them if necessary.

Cut out the motifs and place them on a sheet of marbled paper. Move them around to try out different patterns.

2 When you have decided how to arrange your motifs, mark their positions on the paper with a pencil. Then photocopy enough of the motifs to decorate the entire sheet of marbled paper. Cut them out, leaving a margin of at least 1 inch around the edges. Then, using low-tack masking tape, secure the motifs to the paper, face down, in the marked positions.

Moisten a cotton ball with lighter fluid, then gently wipe this over the back of each motif. Let the lighter fluid evaporate, then rub over the back of the motif with a wooden spatula.

3 Lift up the photocopied motif, then repeat the procedure in all the positions you have marked, using a fresh photocopy each time.

Once the entire piece of marbled paper has been covered with the designs, dab the motifs with some white watercolor paint to create highlights and produce a three-dimensional effect. To finish, spray the paper lightly with fixative.

HANDY TIPS!

To create the effect of old paper, arrange the motifs geometrically. You can do this by choosing what kind of pattern you are going to create – for example, lines, diagonals, or zigzags – and marking the positions of the motifs with a pencil. Victorian-style motifs work well with this type of design.

CRAFT WRAPPING PAPER

This hardworking brown paper has a long history and is very well-traveled; along the way it has been used to protect notebooks and line shelves, as well as wrap parcels for mailing. Craft paper is now back in fashion and can be found in a range of appealing colors.

1 Buy a few rolls or large sheets of craft paper in different colors, for example lilac, yellow, white, and blue, which you can use to create gift bags or wrapping paper. Choose some little figures for your motifs and photocopy them, enlarging them to fit the item you want to decorate. Cut out the motifs.

2 Position your motifs face down on the craft paper and secure them with low-tack masking tape. Then transfer the designs onto the craft paper by rubbing a cotton ball moistened with lighter fluid over the reverse side of each motif. Be careful not to soak the cotton ball too much as craft paper is not very absorbent, and the ink from the photocopy might smudge.

Press the back of the photocopy with the palm of your hand. Once the lighter fluid is dry, rub over the back of the photocopy with a wooden spatula, without applying too much pressure. Lift off the photocopy and leave to dry completely.

3 Next, prepare some watercolor paint. Dilute a light color to begin with, and paint over the whole motif in this color using a fine brush. The paint will collect where no ink has been transferred onto the paper.

Let the paint dry, then repeat the process several times to thicken the color.

Once the design is dry, fix it with charcoal fixative spray or matte varnish. If you like, you can repeat the process using a different color, but still keeping the paint within the motif. To finish, spray the paper lightly with fixative.

HANDY TIPS!

If you choose large-sized sheets of craft paper, you will be able to place several motifs in a row. When decorating gift bags, you can use a single motif on the front and back, placed in the middle or to one side, or you can reproduce the same motif lots of times so that it is dotted all over the surface.

Using lots of color and a few fantasy figures, you can transform a plain paper bag into something special, and then fill it with toys, candies, and gifts for someone special.

1 Save any interesting paper bags in different colors and textures, gleaned from your shopping trips, so that you can transform them into unique gift bags. Decide on a decorating theme and choose suitable motifs. Photocopy the motifs, then cut them out, allowing a margin of at least 1 inch around the edges.

2 Place a photocopied motif face down in the middle of a bag and secure it with low-tack masking tape. Moisten a cotton ball with a little lighter fluid and wipe it gently over the back of the motif, holding it firmly in place. Using an embossing tool or a wooden spatula, rub over the motif, pressing hard and holding the motif to keep it from moving.

3 Lift off the photocopy to reveal the transferred motif. Then touch up the motif, if necessary, with some acrylic paint or a felt-tip marker. Spray with a little fixative to complete.

HANDY TIPS!

Lighter fluid quickly evaporates, so you need to work fast. The more porous the paper is, the quicker you need to complete the transfer, keeping the photocopy damp all the time.

If the bag is made from brown paper and is not very porous, wait for all the lighter fluid to evaporate before pressing the motif down.

ENGRAVED GIFT TAGS

Have fun devising some evocative tags to go with the culinary delights you have created in your kitchen. Alternatively, you can use engraved tags as postcards or invitation cards.

1 You can create motifs on all kinds of paper and card, by engraving them with a pen. Glazed paper and thin pressed-paper board are excellent for this kind of technique; even very thin paper can be used as long as it has a coated surface (for example, waxed paper).

First cover the sheet of paper or board with a layer of acrylic paint or glass paint in the color of your choice. Leave to dry.

2 If you use a light-colored paint, the second coat should be dark, and vice versa. Pour some glass paint for the second coat onto a flat plate. Lightly soak a small sponge in this color, and dab this over the paper or board. Vary how you apply the paint, using sweeping and dabbing motions, to create a patina or mottled effect.

3 Before the paint dries, take a calligraphy pen and draw your motif in the paint. There are several types of calligraphy pen nibs available, which will enable you to obtain a variety of interesting effects. From time to time, use a rag to clean off all the debris that builds up on the pen nib.

Use this technique to create tags for jellies and preserves, postcards, visiting cards, or invitation cards.

HANDY TIPS!

Use a light color for the first coat and a much darker one for the second, to create a good contrast. Work quickly once you have applied the second coat of glass paint. The more the paint dries, the less you will see of the base layer.

Avoid using paper that is very porous because the paint needs to remain on the surface for the engraving to work.

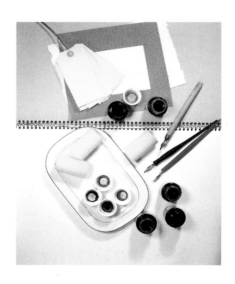

Gold and purple paint create a very festive look. Dress up your paper this Christmas with all kinds of decorative effects.

1 Cut large sheets of paper into bands 4 inches wide. Recycled paper is best because it will enable you to give your friezes an aged appearance.

Pin several bands of paper to a wooden board with thumbtacks or pushpins.

Prepare some wine-colored gouache in a bowl. Paint the bands all over with a soft brush to avoid streaks and leave to dry. Rub the paper all over with a rag.

2 Copy a medallion frieze onto tracing paper with a thick, soft pencil, then transfer it onto the wine-colored paper band by placing it face down and drawing over the outlines. (Each tracing can be used more than once.) Prepare three base colors of gouache: beige, mid-brown, and sepia, earth, or gold. Paint the frieze, beginning with the lightest color and working toward the darkest. Create textured effects by placing dark blobs on one side and light ones on the other. Leave to dry.

To 'age' the paint, rub it lightly with a piece of fine-grade sandpaper. If necessary, sand the motifs too. Spray with fixative to complete.

HANDY TIPS!

Use gouache rather than acrylic paint if you want a powdery finish. When you sand the paint gently for an aged appearance a lovely velvety effect will be produced on the surface.

FABULOUS FABRICS

Beautifully decorated fabrics can completely transform the atmosphere of your home. In this chapter you will discover how to create a host of stunning effects using stencils on a variety of fabrics and other materials. These inspired decorating ideas are all very simple to make, and you'll have lots of fun working on them. What's more, you don't have to throw out your old drapes and window blinds – you can easily modify them for these projects.

In this chapter, you will find examples of drapes, blinds, and screens to decorate, instructions and tips on how to achieve the same look, plus a selection of motifs that will help you to create your very own designs. All you need to do is to follow the technical instructions given in the first section, and reproduce the motifs you have chosen from the selection in the Motif section by tracing or photocopying them. You'll be amazed at how quickly you can bring a dramatic new look to your home.

FABULOUS FABRICS PROJECTS

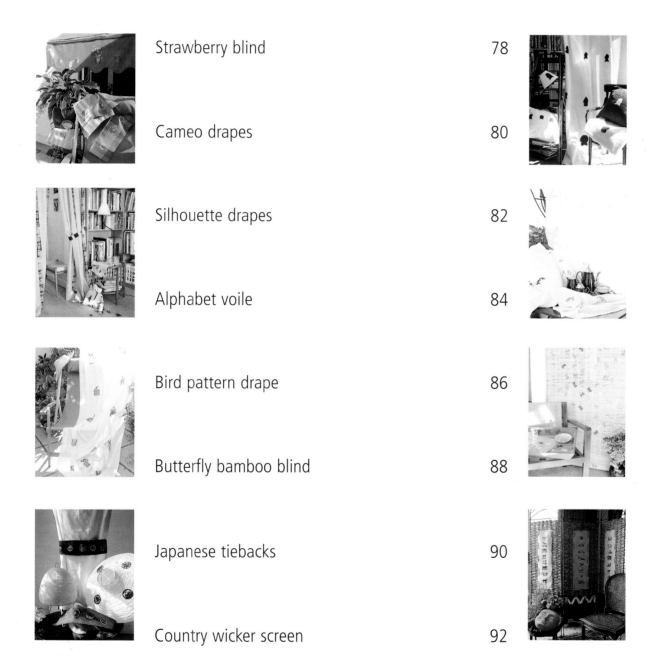

EQUIPMENT

Here is a list of the tools and materials you will need to enable you to successfully complete the projects on the following pages.

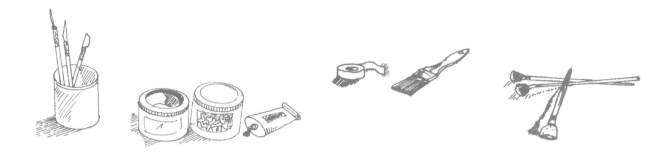

For the strawberry blind

- A colored fabric blind

- A pair of scissors

- Masking tape

- Cotton balls

- A can of lighter fluid

- A wooden spatula or spoon

- A fine brush

- White fabric paint

For the cameo drapes

- A pair of heavy, thick cotton drapes, with tabs

- A pair of scissors

- A spray-can of repositional remount adhesive

- Thin black felt

- A spray-can of adhesive suitable for securing fabric

- A sewing needle

- Black sewing thread

- Paper-backed iron-on fusible web

For the silhouette drapes

- A pair of brightly colored, plain cotton drapes, with tabs

- Some fabric paint

- A sponge paint roller, about 4 inches wide

- Acetate sheets for photocopying or plastic stencil film

- A craft knife with spare blades

- A cutting mat

- A spray-can of repositional remount adhesive

- Masking tape

- A flat-ended round stenciling brush

For the alphabet voile

- Fine voile, muslin, or gauze drapes

- Tracing paper

- A pair of scissors

- Masking tape

- Cotton balls

- A can of lighter fluid

- A wooden spatula or spoon

For the bird pattern drape

- Plain, cream cotton drapes

- A sheet of glazed pressed-paper board, ⅛ inch thick

- A cutting mat

- A craft knife with spare blades

- Fabric paint

- A spray-can of repositional remount adhesive

- A flat wide brush

- A pair of scissors

- Masking tape

- Cotton balls

- A can of lighter fluid

- A wooden spatula or spoon

- A fine brush

For the butterfly bamboo blind

- Plastic stencil film

- An indelible felt-tip marker

- A cutting mat

- A craft knife with spare blades

- Artists' acrylics

- A spray-can of repositional remount adhesive

- A bamboo roller blind

- A flat-ended round stenciling brush

- A spray-can of matte water-based varnish

For the
Japanese tiebacks

- Wide tiebacks made of plain-colored fabric

- A pair of scissors

- Masking tape

- Cotton balls

- A can of lighter fluid

- A wooden spatula or spoon

- Silver fabric paint

- A very fine brush

For the country
wicker screen

- Artists' canvas

- A pair of scissors

- A tape measure

- An HB pencil

- A hole punch

- Masking tape

- Cotton balls

- A can of lighter fluid

- A wooden spatula or spoon

- A palette

- A tube of oil paint in the color of your choice

- Quick-drying varnish

- A fine brush

- A wicker screen

- A curved upholstery needle

- Raffia

A few useful tips

- If you plan to buy new drapes, buy the ready-to-hang kind. There are many different types available, ranging from sheer voile to thick heavy drapes, with a variety of fittings, including tabs, eyelets, and straps to tie round the curtain rod.

- Choose plain drapes rather than patterned ones, so that any decoration will be easily visible.

- Avoid velvet and brocade drapes. Smooth fabrics are easier to decorate.

- To make successful transfers:
  - It's best to choose a thick, tightly woven fabric so that you can transfer more intricate motifs. If the fabric is coarse with an open weave, the transfer will be more difficult and the motif will have to be simpler.
  - Keep the fabric stretched. You can attach the part you are decorating to a board with some thumbtacks.

  - Wipe cotton balls soaked in lighter fluid over the photocopy quickly, before it evaporates.
  - The wooden spatula you use to smooth down the motif must be rounded so that it does not tear the photocopy.
  - Always place the fabric on a sheet of cardboard so that the ink does not run.

- For the stencils:
  - Your paint should not be too runny or too dry.
  - Never load too much paint onto your brush, and dab it gently over the stencil to prevent paint running underneath.
  - To prevent the stencil from slipping, secure it with some repositional remount adhesive, sprayed on the back.

THE TECHNIQUES USED

Strawberry blind: painted transfers
Cameo drapes: appliquéd motifs
Silhouette drapes: stenciling
Alphabet voile: transfers
Bird pattern drape: transfers and stenciling
Butterfly bamboo blind: stenciling
Japanese tiebacks: painted transfers
Country wicker screen: painted transfers

STRAWBERRY BLIND

Give your kitchen window blind a fresh, summery feel by sprinkling it with young strawberries or other young fruits and vegetables, just like those growing in your garden.

1 To create a summery atmosphere, choose a blind in a color like russet, blue, green, or yellow.

Select motifs of fruits or vegetables from the Motif section. Photocopy the motifs, enlarging them to a size of approximately 6 inches square.

2 Cut out the photocopies leaving a margin around each image, place them face down on your blind and secure them with a piece of masking tape.

Soak a cotton ball with lighter fluid, and dab this over the back of the photocopied motifs to moisten the paper. Then, using a wooden spatula, rub over the back of each motif, holding it steady on the fabric.

3 Lift up the photocopies, to reveal the transferred motifs on the fabric.

Using a fine brush, fill in the blank areas of the motif with some white fabric paint. Leave to dry, then press with an iron to fix the color.

HANDY TIPS!

Leave some space between each motif so that the design does not become too cluttered.

It's best to choose motifs where the graphics and themes are of the same style.

Don't choose a blind with very thin fabric, or the sun shining through will make the decorations invisible.

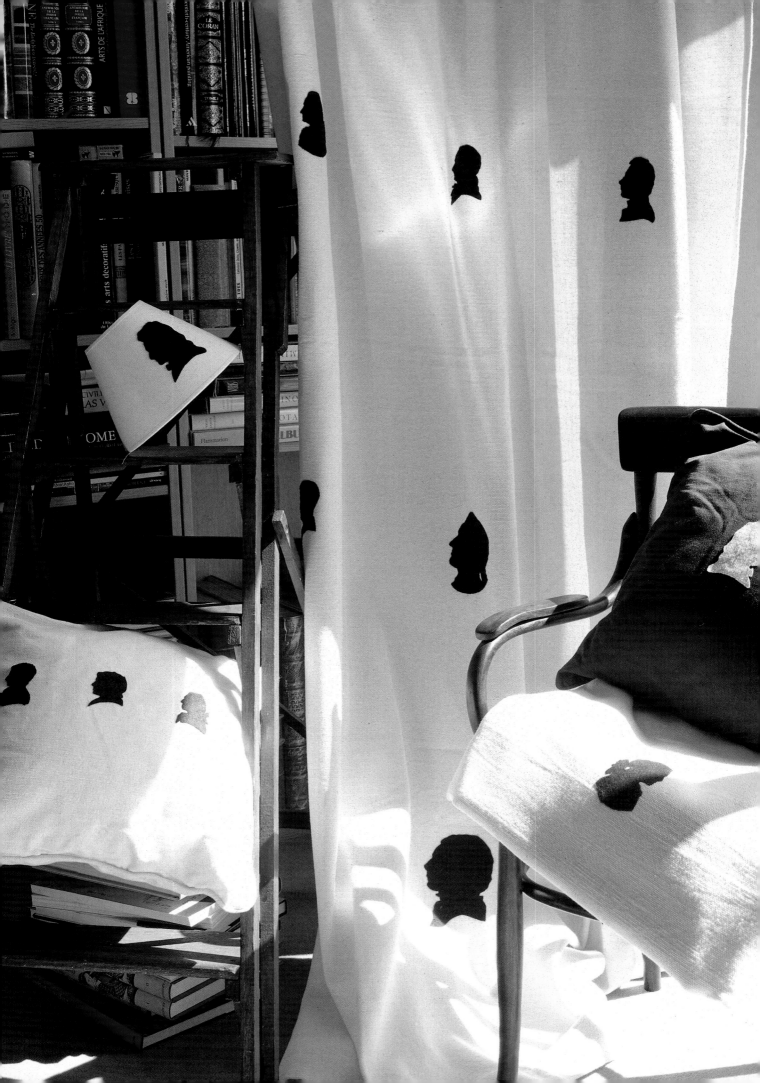

Use a simple, bold motif to create a striking effect in a favorite corner of a room, where you can sit with all your familiar objects around you.

1 Choose a pair of thick, heavy cotton drapes with tabs. Then select some black silhouettes of faces that are simple to cut out. Photocopy these faces, enlarging them to different sizes. Prepare the same number of motifs for each drape.

When you have photocopied as many faces as you need, cut them out and place them flat on the drapes so that you can check that the black shapes form a balanced and harmonious pattern.

2 Take the cutouts one by one, and spray some repositional remount adhesive on the reverse side. Stick each motif on a piece of thin black felt and cut out the shape, following the outline of the photocopy (if you are using fusible web, read step 3 first). Then remove the photocopy and place the felt face down in its position on the drape. Repeat the process until all your shapes are ready.

3 You can attach the felt motifs to the drapes in two ways. One way is to stick them on lightly with aerosol fabric adhesive and then sew round the edges with black thread. However, this method is time-consuming and the stitches show on the back of the drape. The second option is to use paper-backed iron-on fusible web. Fuse the fusible web to the back of the felt before you start cutting out the shapes. After cutting out the shapes, peel off the paper backing, then apply each motif to the drape by fusing it in place on the drape with the iron.

HANDY TIPS!

Choose other fabrics instead of the felt if you prefer. Fusible web can be used to stop raw edges from fraying.

Make sure you place the motifs in such a way that they don't all disappear into the folds of the drapes.

SILHOUETTE DRAPES

Create a pair of stylish striped drapes using a little imagination and some fun silhouette motifs.

1 Stretch out a pair of brightly colored, plain cotton drapes with tabs on the floor. Pour some fabric paint into a dish; here, we used black but you can use any color you like. Dilute the paint slightly.

Then, using a medium-size paint roller, paint a vertical stripe on the drapes from top to bottom in one movement. Press only lightly to begin with, and then as you go down press harder on the roller, to maintain the stripe right to the end. Allow the paint to dry, then repeat the process to paint other stripes in the same way. You can make the stripes appear bold or faint, as desired.

2 Choose a motif and photocopy or trace it onto a sheet of acetate or plastic stencil film. Cut out the motif with a craft knife, on a cutting mat, to make a stencil. Then spray the back of the stencil with a fine mist of repositional remount adhesive and stick it to the fabric; alternatively, you can use masking tape to secure it.

3 Pour some fabric paint in a dish and dilute it slightly. Then, using a round flat-ended stenciling brush, apply the color, little by little to the stencil placed on the drape. Take care to work slowly, holding the stencil steady against the fabric and applying the paint in several light coats, one after the other. Let the motif dry as you go along and make sure that the paint goes right to the edge of the stencil. Once the paint is completely dry, you can start on your next motif. Lastly, fix the paint by pressing with an iron.

HANDY TIPS!

Check from time to time that the back of the stencil is not stained with paint, and clean it regularly so that you don't get any marks on the fabric.

To fix the fabric paint safely, place a cloth between the drape and the iron.

ALPHABET VOILE

A floaty drape lets the light and the scents from the garden gently drift into your home. Make it look even more elegant with a few charming motifs. It's as easy as ABC!

1 Choose a drape made from a light floaty fabric, such as voile, muslin, or gauze. Because these fabrics are so light, they create a fluid and airy effect. Select some small motifs, such as letters or numbers, that can be dotted over the drape at random. Don't choose intricate motifs because you will only get a faint transfer on the gauze; the basic shapes will be recognizable but the details will not show up clearly.

2 For the fabric motifs, first photocopy the numbers or letters onto a sheet of tracing paper. Then put this photocopy face down on the photocopier glass in order to reverse the image. This will enable you to get the letters and numbers the right way around when you transfer them onto the fabric. Repeat this operation several times, enlarging or reducing the motifs as you go.

3 Cut out a number or letter, leaving a border of at least 1 inch around it. Place the photocopy face down on the fabric and secure it with masking tape, taking care not to cover the motif. Moisten a cotton ball with lighter fluid and wipe this over the back of the photocopy. Rub the back of the motif with a wooden spatula, keeping the motif and fabric absolutely flat as you are working.

Lift up the photocopy and leave the transferred motif to dry. Repeat this process as many times as you like, until you have a nice spread of motifs on the drape.

BIRD PATTERN DRAPE

When temperatures soar, it's time to retire behind a chirpy bird-patterned drape for a Mediterranean-style siesta.

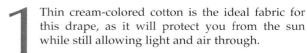

1 Thin cream-colored cotton is the ideal fabric for this drape, as it will protect you from the sun while still allowing light and air through.

Take your length of fabric and at 16-inch intervals mark a 2-inch square, 2 inches from the edge. Repeat across the fabric at even intervals.

To make a stencil, place a sheet of glazed board on a cutting mat and cut it into an 8-inch square. Cut a 4-inch square out of the middle using a craft knife.

Dilute some fabric paint in a bowl.

2 Spray repositional remount adhesive onto the back of the square stencil and place it on the length of drape at one of the marked positions. Press it firmly onto the fabric. Dip a flat, wide brush into the paint and sweep it over the stencil from top to bottom to achieve the textured effect shown. Remove the stencil and leave to dry.

3 Select some bird motifs and photocopy them so that they are all roughly the same size. Cut out the photocopies, then position them face down on the fabric, one above each painted square. Secure with masking tape. Moisten a cotton ball with lighter fluid and wipe this over the back of each motif, then rub the back of the motif with a wooden spatula.

Remove the photocopies and allow to dry. Then color the transfers with fabric paint applied with a fine brush.

Fix the paint by pressing the motifs with an iron.

HANDY TIPS!

The paint should not be too liquid or it will run on the fabric.

Apply your paint to the stencil in single swift stroke.

BUTTERFLY BAMBOO BLIND

For a touch of sheer frivolity, how about decorating a window blind with a host of dainty butterflies that look as though they've just fluttered in from outside?

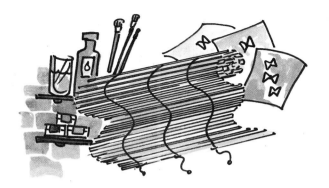

1 Choose four butterfly designs and trace them onto plastic stencil film using an indelible felt-tip marker. Place the motifs on a cutting mat and use a craft knife to cut them out carefully following their contours.

Avoid a lot of fine detail, because the plastic stencil might split after being handled numerous times.

Cut out a spare stencil for each design.

2 Mix several shades of acrylic paint in separate containers. Choose the colors depending on the atmosphere you want to create, for example, a bright multicolored effect, or a subtle graduated effect with four shades of the same color. Use one color for each stencil.

Spray repositional remount adhesive onto the back of each of the four stencils and carefully stick them to the bamboo blind.

Make sure that all parts of each stencil are firmly in contact with the bamboo.

3 Load a round flat-ended stenciling brush with a small amount of paint and gently dab it onto the first stencil. If the slats are rounded, use your brush at different angles to make sure that all the wood is colored. If the slats are flat, apply your paint in the normal manner.

Change the paint shade and paint the second stencil, then the third and the fourth. Repeat this process as many times as you like over the blind to cover it either partially or completely. Another idea is to use the same stencil all the time but vary the color.

Leave the blind to dry flat, and then spray on a coat of matte varnish.

HANDY TIPS!

To partition a room, or filter the light, choose a blind made from wooden slats, either unvarnished or tinted and varnished.

This stenciling technique can be used on all kinds of venetian-style blinds with wooden slats.

JAPANESE TIEBACKS

Decorate some tiebacks with exquisite silver filigree motifs to complement your drapes and give your decor a really professional touch.

1 Choose a pair of tiebacks made of plain fabric and preferably fairly wide. You can use paler or brighter shades to match your decor and the color of your drapes.

Select some circular Japanese motifs, with a similar shape and theme, such as flowers, geometric patterns, or astrology symbols. Enlarge them on a photocopier to obtain a maximum diameter of 4 inches. Cut out the motifs, leaving at least 1 inch all around each one so that you can secure them to the tieback.

2 Place the photocopied motifs face down on the fabric and secure in place with masking tape. Make sure you get the first motif right in the center so that you can position the other ones correctly afterward.

Wipe the back of the photocopy with a cotton ball moistened with lighter fluid, then rub the back of the image with a wooden spatula, pressing hard and evenly, so that the motif transfers well onto the fabric.

Lift up the photocopies and leave the transferred motifs to dry completely.

3 Next, prepare some silver-colored fabric paint. Choose thick paint, preferably in a tube and dilute it only slightly; in this way, it will hide the color of the fabric quickly.

Using a very fine brush, apply the paint to the motif in the places where the ink has not stained the fabric. Leave to dry and, if necessary, apply a second layer of paint.

Leave to dry, then fix the motifs by pressing them with an iron.

HANDY TIPS!

When painting fabric, always allow the first coat to dry before applying the second for a neater finish.

Work carefully to avoid paint runs on the fabric which would ruin the distinct shapes of the motifs.

COUNTRY WICKER SCREEN

A screen like this is a real asset in a room, especially when decorated with canvas panels covered with country-style motifs.

1 Cut a rectangle of artists' canvas for each panel of your screen (here we have three); the dimensions of the rectangles will depend on the size of panels in your screen.

Using a tape measure, mark the positions of the holes to be made every 4 inches around each piece of canvas. Next, make the holes with the hole punch (these will eventually be used to attach the panels to the screen).

2 Choose a series of motifs. Photocopy them, enlarging or reducing them so that they are all of a similar size; make sure that they remain clear and distinct. Mark the position of each motif on the canvas rectangles with a pencil. Then cut out the motifs, leaving a margin of at least 1 inch around each motif, and place them on the canvas, creating a balanced effect with the shapes.

Once the individual positions of the motifs have been determined, secure them face down with some masking tape. Wipe a cotton ball moistened with lighter fluid over the back of each photocopy, then rub the back of the image with a wooden spatula. Remove the photocopies, and leave the transferred motifs until completely dry.

3 On a palette, mix some oil paint in the color of your choice together with some quick-drying varnish. Paint all the motifs with the paint and varnish mixture using a fine brush; leave to dry.

Lastly, stitch the canvas panels to the screen using a curved upholstery needle and some lengths of raffia.

HANDY TIPS!

If your screen is made from beige canvas, you can transfer the motifs directly onto the canvas and then paint them.

For screens made from wood or natural fiber, use separate panels of artists' canvas, and then attach them when they are complete.

Choose motifs from the same theme or use a motley collection for variety.

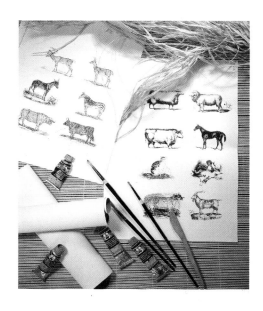

MOTIFS

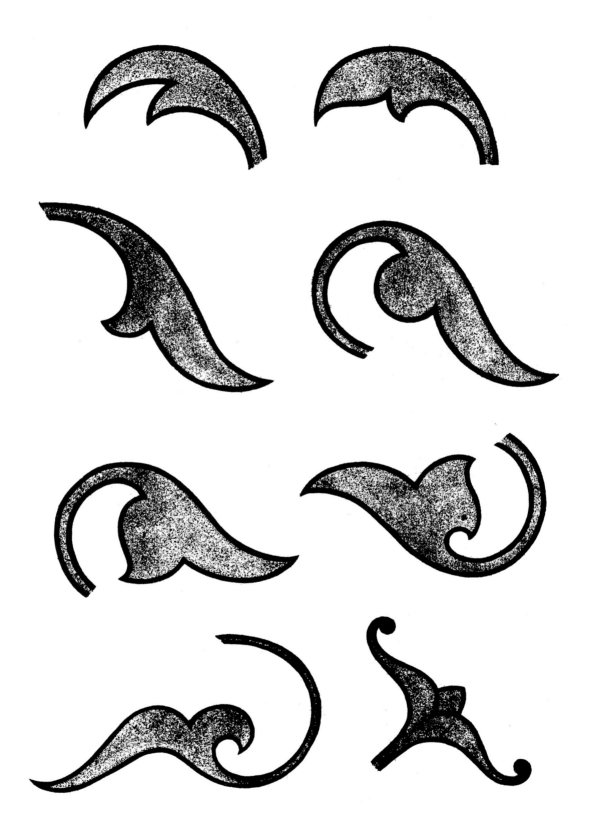

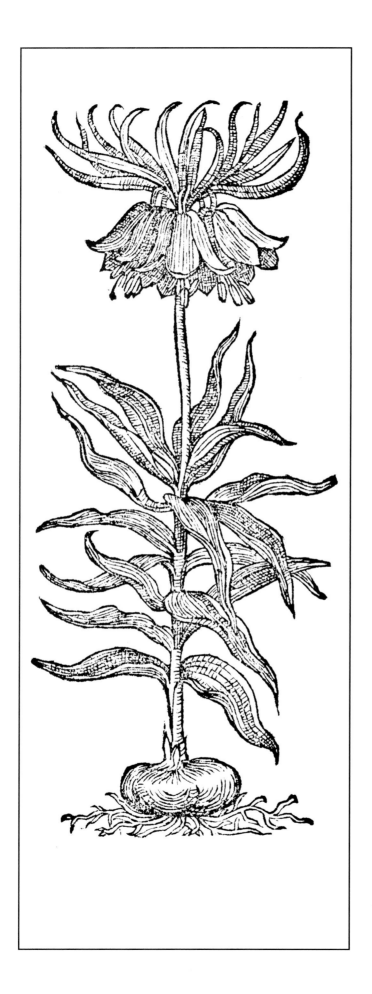
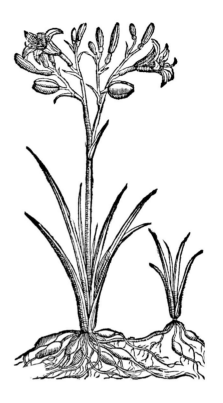

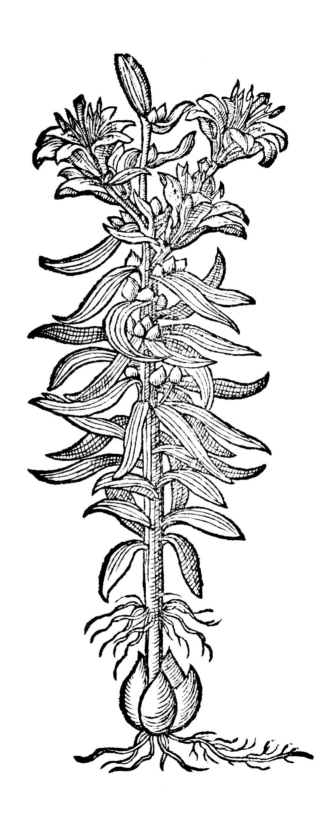

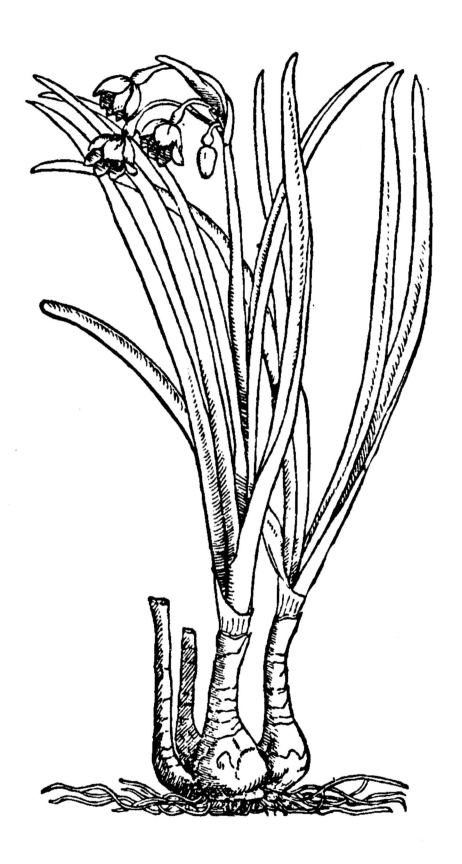

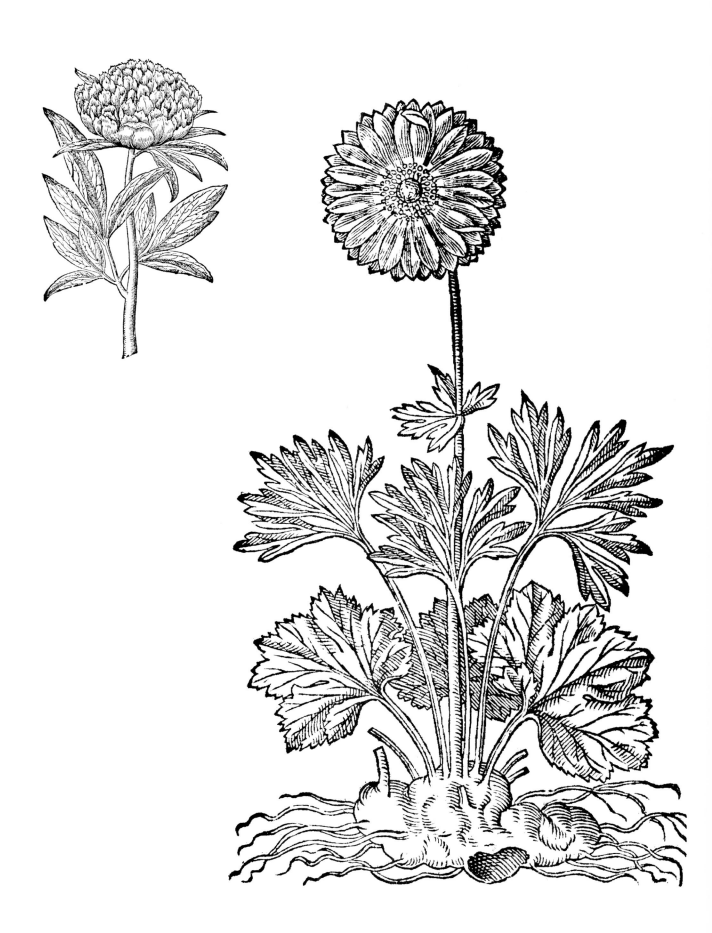

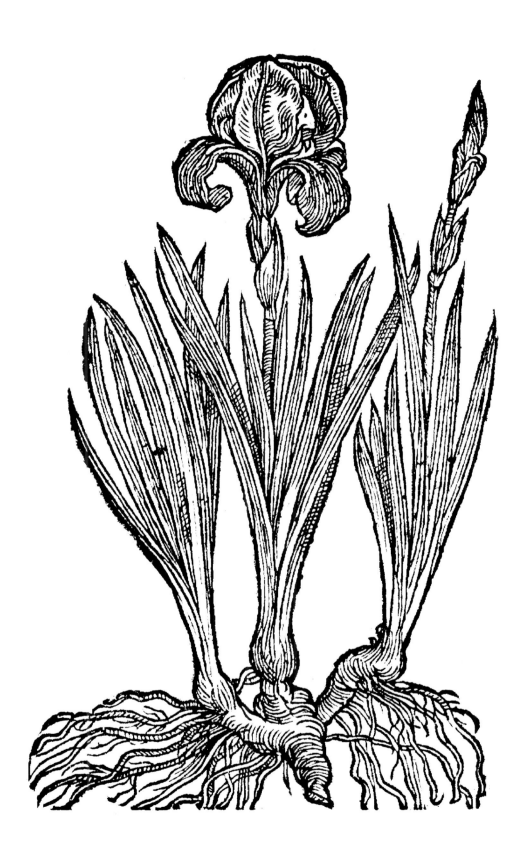

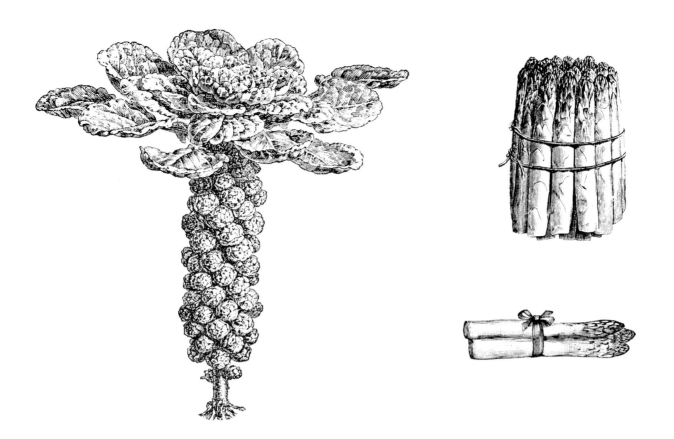

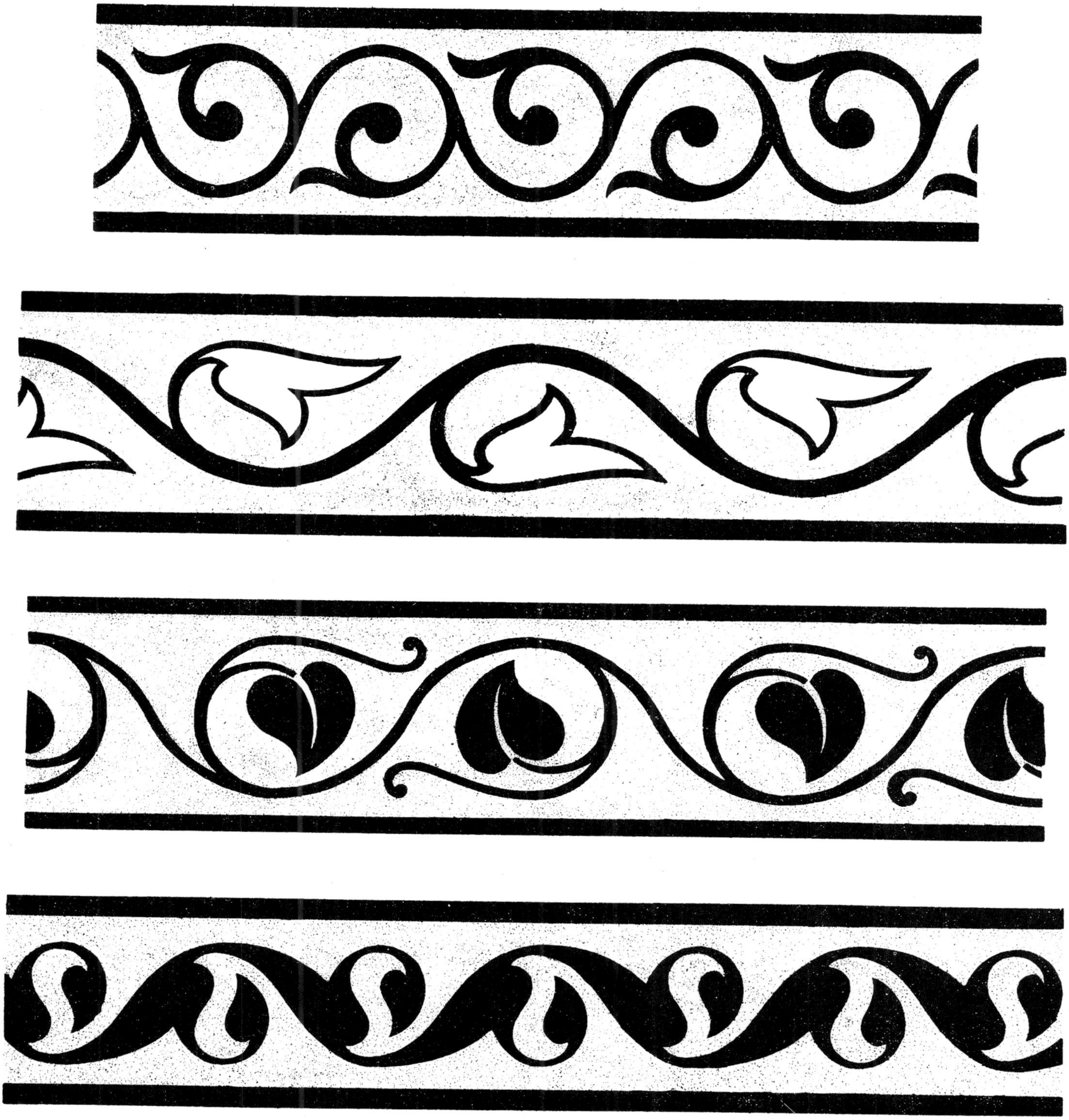

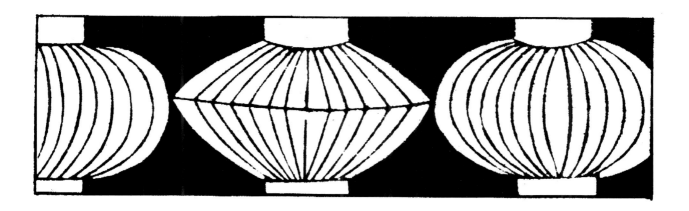

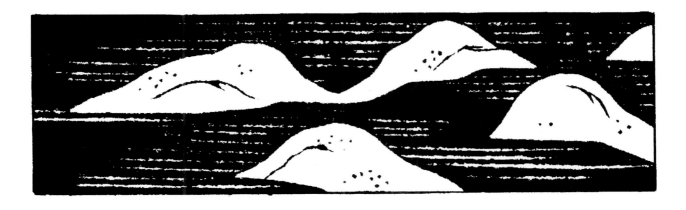

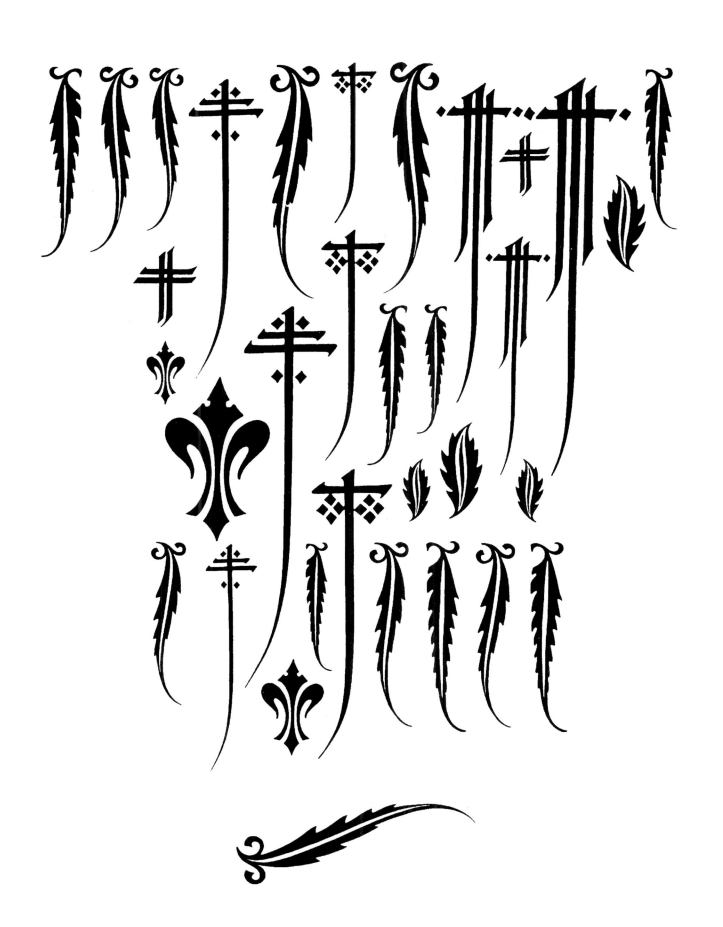

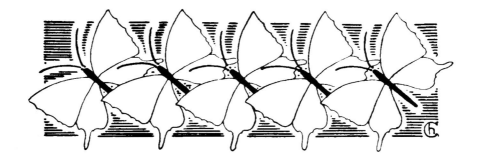

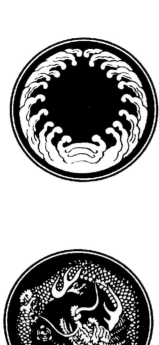

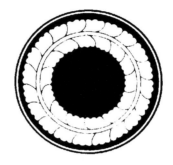

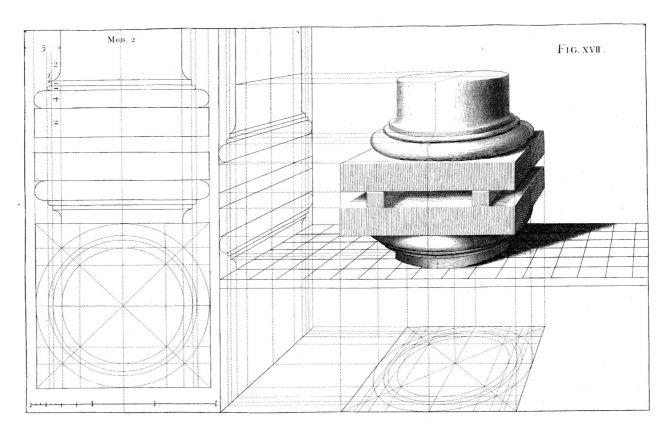

Mod. 2

FIG. XVII.

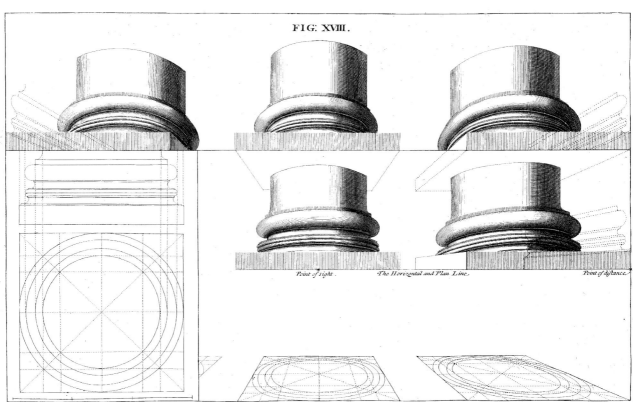

FIG. XVIII.

Point of sight.   The Horizontal and Plan Line.   Point of distance.

 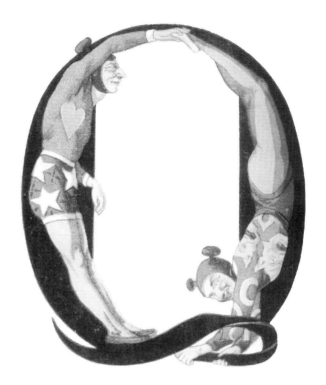

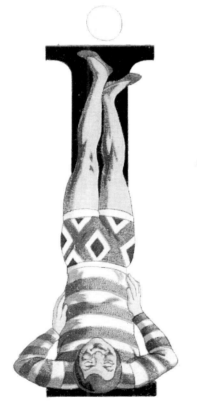 

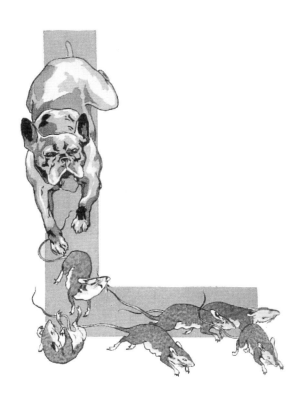

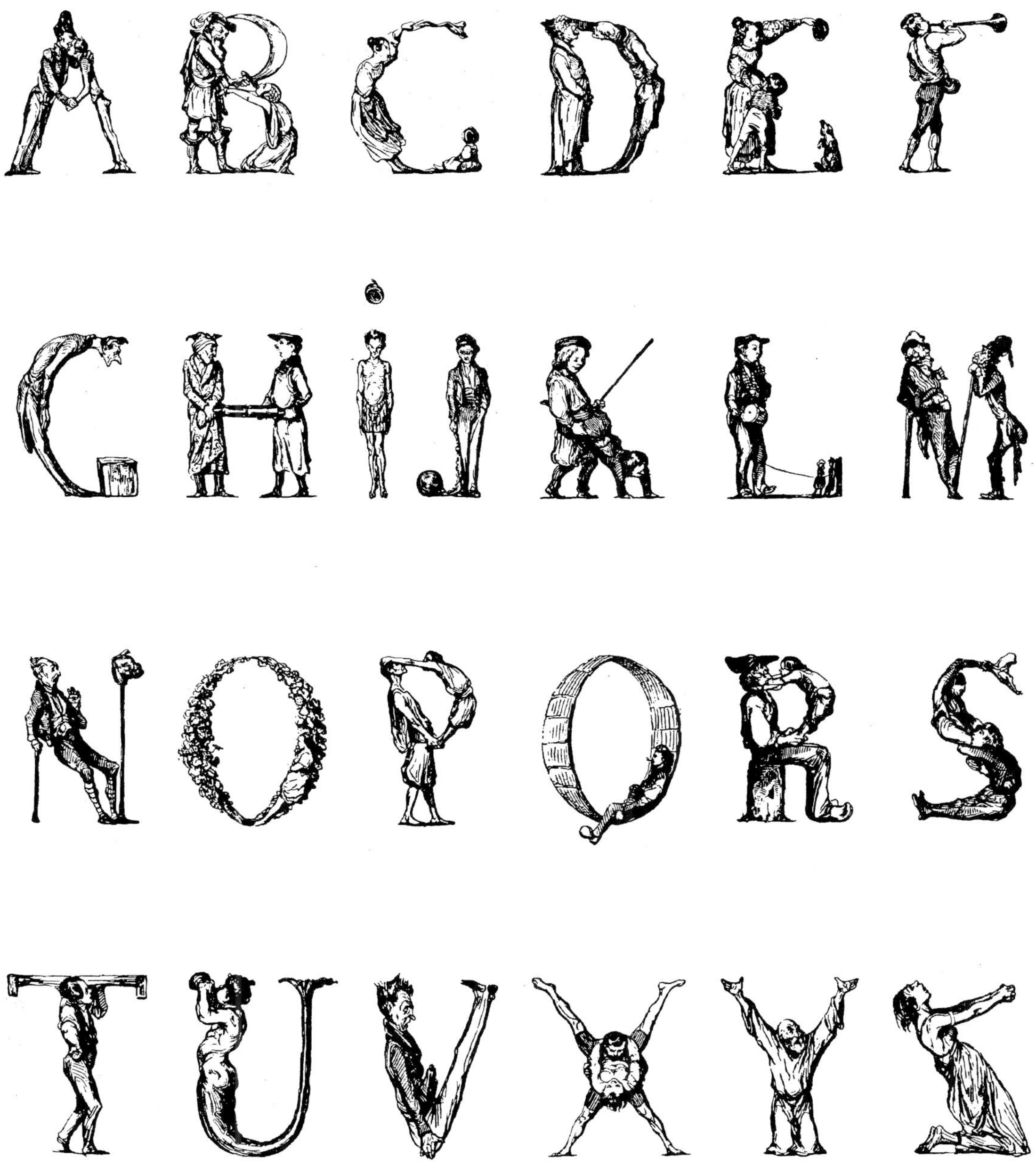
ABCDEF
GHIJKLM
NOPQRS
TUVXYZ

A B C D E F

G H I J K L

M N O P Q

R S T U V

W X Y Z Œ

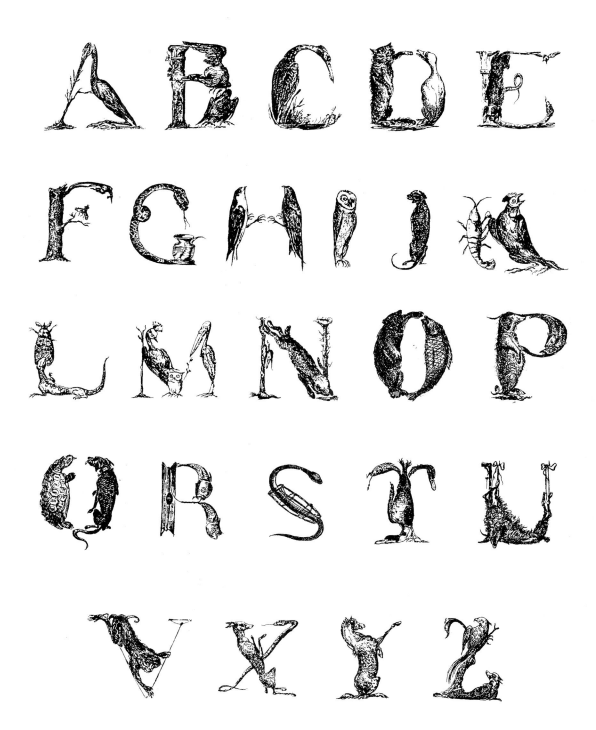

1234567890

1 2 3 4 5
6 7 8 9 0

1 2 3 4 5
6 7 8 9 0

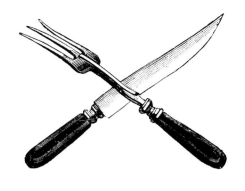